EVEN THE DARK

Crab Orchard Series in Poetry
OPEN COMPETITION AWARD

EVEN THE DARK

poems by

LESLIE WILLIAMS

Crab Orchard Review &
Southern Illinois University Press
Carbondale

Southern Illinois University Press
www.siupress.com

22 21 20 19   4 3 2 1

Cover illustration: "Light and shade portrait of a vulture, bird of
   prey," cropped, by Wendy Corniquet; Shutterstock

The Crab Orchard Series in Poetry is a joint publishing
   venture of Southern Illinois University Press and *Crab
   Orchard Review*. This series has been made possible by the
   generous support of the Office of the President of Southern
   Illinois University and the Office of the Vice Chancellor
   for Academic Affairs and Provost at Southern Illinois
   University Carbondale.

Editor of the Crab Orchard Series in Poetry: Jon Tribble
Judge for the 2018 Open Competition Award: Allison Joseph

       Library of Congress Cataloging-in-Publication Data
Names: Williams, Leslie, 1967– author.
Title: Even the dark / Leslie Williams.
Description: Carbondale : Southern Illinois University Press,
   2019. | Series: Crab Orchard series in poetry
Identifiers: LCCN 2019000967 | ISBN 9780809337491
   (paperback) | ISBN 9780809337507 (ebook)
Subjects: | BISAC: POETRY / American / General.
Classification: LCC PS3623.I5585 A6 2019 | DDC
   811/.6—dc23 LC record available at https://lccn.loc.
   gov/2019000967

Printed on recycled paper. ♻

This paper meets the requirements of ANSI/NISO Z39.48-
   1992 (Permanence of Paper). ∞

for my neighbors

God, as Brother Giles said, is a great mountain of corn from which man, like a sparrow, takes a grain of wheat: yet even that grain of wheat, which is as much as we can carry away, contains all the essentials of our life. We are to carry it carefully and eat it gratefully: remembering with awe the majesty of the mountain from which it comes.

—Evelyn Underhill, *The School of Charity*

CONTENTS

✒

CREWELWORK

With more persistent stitchery
I might breach the red intelligence of berries
taking French-knot shapes among embroidered
leaves, or bring a spirit hovering
in the satin-stitch of a hummingbird's
small throat; while outlining a dragonfly
I may divine its mythic origin
in Dragon—fiery, winged, then tricked
into an insect's form, but keeping
flashes of the fabled—like all of us
who come from far, bringing stories
of vain passions once pursued. What I came to
as a child, pulled up outside the needlework
shop: a window with such breezy sheers
that I fell endlessly through, my hopeless thread
a tangle under sewing hoops, snag and snarl
of vivid yarn the way our world looks,
and then the thrill to hear the shopkeeper
say: Be still. It is the fabric's finished side
that's visible from heaven.

ELM

At an outdoor concert once I lay in a gully cracked
with stars and felt intensely sorry I would not always
be around to take it in, to try out other lives, say
in a split-level under stardust, mother-in-law's tongue
growing dusty in the window, a visiting Buick
in the driveway, pillows and maps on the long
backseat. What gets me about fall is the chance
of going over a mountain—the snap that anything might
come to pass—and the violent absence of a friend,
who in days before had been knocking, whispery
at neighbors' doors until she and her son went savagely

missing from the earth, gone from every comfortable
routine, missing simply walking into grocery stores
among the beautiful hills of fruit. And today, a glorious
fall day, the kind to put your eyes out, radiant
solidity of brick—why could she not feel the dirt-floor
certainty that she would always want to wait and see,
hold out for one more violet, just-past-sunset
sky surrounding any ramifying tall tree, the dark
branches saying *here I am* and not a bit sorry.

THE GREAT MIRROR

Every morning the jeweler opens
her safe, retrieves the rubies

to fasten around brushed velvet necks
in the window, while in other shopfronts

merchants mix the newest salts with more
traditional meats—I should be caught

out squandering this abundant day, punished
as were the Puritans who coasted

or fowled or took tobacco, failing to *improve
the time*—to turn all whiles

to good account. When I still had a generous
three hours I didn't ask the questions

I needed most to ask: for a glass of water
or who the Desert Mothers were, or how I might

fulfill my purpose here, but sat in the sunny café
reading magazines: about the telescopes trained

on places where Big Bang atoms are still racing
outward, from long before the time of Vincent

of Beauvais, who swore that fresh warm goat's
blood would shatter rubies, diamonds

too; from before the time of priests
who salted infants against demons

by blowing three times on their faces,
placing salt upon their tongues. From before

the time of Saint Augustine, who would
often pray: *Lord, shield the joyous.*

THINKING OF GOD'S GOODNESS
WHILE THE TEN-YEAR-OLD NEIGHBOR IS SUFFERING

Standing at my sink eating an entire package of salami, I know God is good, my God, but I watched the girl in penguin pajamas make her way slowly down their front walk, going for more chemicals to be poured into her small body, where things have gone rapidly and aggressively wrong. God, if I am full part anguish, what multiple are they? The parents, their only child, the apple, the amen. Lost from fifth grade, bicycle, library, lake. Just at Halloween she and a friend were skipping house to house, stuffing their pumpkin buckets full. I'm remembering the first days after having my baby, when I'd rouse for a minute and not remember he was here. Does the mother have days like that, waking up and briefly not knowing her daughter is sick? Not thinking anything? And is that merciful, a moment's forgetting, or is it worse when the fresh fact comes smashing through? I do believe a sickness can be rebuked, vanish with all the darkest days; that they could return to singing. That one day this devastation could be shadow only, a conquering. Where even the dark is not dark to see. My God can do this but my God might not.

THE YOUNGEST OCEAN

It's a handmade raft I live on,
slowly gathering sense
of its limited dimensions.

What came first: heart of gold
or body of glass, being alone
or liking it?

Water tables, ice sheets, river beds,
a priest or the listening
milk or bread?

When a woman is dead
her memory is small fish bones
or the rabbit's foot

found when cleaning house,
down to one drinking glass
and a summer book,

down to the vintage scent
of gardenia carried out to sea,
out to the raft of three days

with a broken mast,
alone with a harmonica
and the only song I knew.

Each time they leave the house I worry *this is it.*
The last plank of hope, burned hard into the pit.
All the timber the bridge is built with, torched, by
grim words from world experts who go home to
their own linens. The priest says *if she were my child
I'd want prayers for healing until last breath.* The priest
says *what about you?* I'm overwhelmed: the sublime
perfumed featherings of lilac, never knowing what
to do for others but letting swallows make a home
here because I can spare the eaves.

SO MANY DAYS ARE BEAUTIES

June sun invigorating widescale greening lawns
and treats stored up inside the house:
marshmallows or orange sherbet.

Putting our boats in the Charles today
I have a problem looking for the lesson
in everything, trying to be the good.

On the plane I was trying to help the mother
who struggled with her howling infant, screaming
toddler, spilling diaper bag, bulky booster seat,

because when I was young I'd often wished
someone would step in for me, but the woman said:
Could you stop, please?

I've seen the austere snowscape outside the neighbors' lamplit living room. I've seen the lawn, the one trumpet lily blooming. Yesterday before the storm the mother drove in and closed the garage, returning (I assume) with the secret spice for making stew or something good. In my own kitchen I'm trying to justify my curious gaze, make their story fit my catalog of special sights: the monk scraping rice bowls in an empty hall, or a girl waving madly to my train from poppy fields. I have defiled my possibility, intensely cold and sunny afternoons when my babies woke from naps and I could have invited my neighbor and her baby over for coffee and a chat. I could have asked her sooner before anything was wrong.

FOX IN THE YARD

Burned she is in mind
or chosen, the one sighting I always
go back to—living orange amulet, alert

unhurried stride—when she moves off
I call her under the willow, without
permanence of answer—

I'm called away from windows,
my little son asking why God made sickness
as he races around the kitchen,

jubilant about an invitation, a friend's
birthday, my sons my antidote
for complacency, my fox

a medicine with which I am briefly
allowed to see—*if Thou art so lovely
in thy creatures, how exceeding ravishing*

Thou must be—but what if the story's
just elaborate invention, a made-up
Upper Room where everyone's at prayer

more earnestly than I? I'm always sputtering
at ironing board, with apron string,
battling my noonday demons

for a divine gaze to fall on, shatter me—
I'd believe in kneeling here:
my heaven, hot summer evening

surrounded by superfused green,
harbored from the hurricane before
an uneasy dawning *the fox was sick*—You

there, every little thing all right, playing
the song till dark.
The fox is burned in mind

from so far back—prayer bead on worry
chain, the easy loping pace that accelerates
then is *gone,* for years. Can't stop the name

called under the willow, with only
the rarest clarity of answer—oh absences!
I'm trusting you.

LATTERLY

Lord, I do
expect you

in the coming-for-to-seek-me
in a humming afternoon

when home
in every corner will be
radical in comfort.

What's a life for? Mine's been
seeking safety mostly,
but there's that thirsting

for the well—to stride,
go forward, feast
on summer fineness,

country wine,
to trust the finest
summers still on vines—

possibly they are not
mine—
but are, for someone,

someone will.
Someone will adore the world,
its exquisite sloop.

SAFE IN THE GROUND

There's nothing more
the certified arborist can do.

He's lopped off diseased
branches, congealed

green wounds with tar.
Waited too long for new leaves.

So all day swinging from a crane
men in diaper-harnesses handle

buzzing saws, then prise the fluted
quick of sycamore stump from earth.

At dusk among the uproots'
knuckling whiteness,

a sylph shivers by the low creek,
buries her dead in rags:

a nursery room dreamer,
a greenhorn, a seed.

Now she's afoot in stony hills:
no dog, no fetching stick, no self.

DON'T WORRY

I shut myself away, became
a thirteenth-century anchoress,
received last rites and died
for every purpose of the world.
Outside they scattered ashes
at the threshold of my cell's sealed door.

I had three windows—parlor,
service portal, squint—and so received
some words and food. I had asked for
wisdom and was granted pain, my body
slowly mortifying in its freezing lake,
no longer able to speak or move.

Then in a rush of welcoming, I heard
where is now an instant of your grief?
Released to boundless open field
in highest health, and can I tell you
everything felt solved. The love
washed in and called me back, kept
calling out to me. Some nights I try

to soothe my worried son
with lullaby riffs on reggae songs,
give him the mellow confidence
all manner of thing will be OK.
He says, "No, Mom. Tomorrow
every little thing's gonna really stink."

The winter gathers strength.
One cold night on city sidewalk
I'm surprised to see a friend through

supermarket windows, filling her basket,
looking sprightly in her red beret. The sight
returns me, makes a perfect dent. I don't hear
myself cry out, but feel the echo of it, after.

COME MAKE YOUR CORACLE

of willow bark,
of bullock hide.
Light the candle and bless
the wax.

I've been calling you
with weaverbirds' song,
ornithology and thorn.

Come running to
the household voice.

I'm laying a picnic,
spreading blankets
for you to sit
before you set out
across the river.

Hear me, believe me.
I want what you want.
You're safe here.

From the deepest part of mind
a recurring doodle kept slouching out,
caught on paper as soon as she got home
from school, the gorgeous whole word *California*
filling up her pages with fat bubble script.
She'd been antic, pinpricked from looking
at maps. Her mother, and others, had stayed up
rocking her. She longed to rise from straitened
places, to rise—can you tell her that is wrong?
She's out on the front walk, night-cool cement,
moon in her notebook, drinking Shasta from a can.
She's in a hand-me-down nightgown
and stretching the sleeves.

IN WHICH THE BREAD CRUMBS WERE EATEN BY BIRDS

Natalie Wharton (1968–1985)

Third grade: desegregated, charmed.
When school got out, our two voices
carried across the wires between
my split-level kingdom and the place

she called from, never seen.
In the remembered clearing, a path
of crumbs: birthday party, pigtails
with plastic baubles, her cotton dress.

She did not die a famous woman.
She did not die even a woman.
Curled eyelashes, black irises, dimples,
honeysuckle voice, she left only

the sifting through, slight mental
ridge of 1985, wound of no understanding
          her mouth, the gun
and how quietly the wake closed over her.

But that was just the way it was for me.

THE FOREST

Off again in wading through the daylilies,
then walking on the narrow path in an attitude

of asking, finding nothing more
than intuition in the wake of napping

with which my life began—as often a life
does not begin at its beginning

but after the years of lying in,
brambled into farthest field

needing foolscap for the cutting
thoughts, lucid gaps in which to dwell

and drink in more of pleasure,
its diminishing returns. It is the pure

I'm gone for, unbreakable
by and with the daily life, stays

stitched inside the day, steady riffs
of marvelment and the occasional decisive

leap—an odd September, just before
the bell, a teacher gave me furtively

the hardbound lesson book, black
with purple-pink and orange purling

behind the title: *Serendipity*—(it was never I
who found the knowledge, it was knowledge

finding me)—my true mysterious
education, so much I want to ask you.

SPRIGGED MUSLIN OF THE HEARTBREAK VOICE

Eleanor Ross Taylor (1920–2011)

I've been sorry
      for the spills, cleaned
because I did not want
      to leave a stain.

When her house went up
      for sale I went in, laid
hands to table, wandered
      her wood floors,

marveled at the cold black stove
      the kitchen held,
brick hearth darkened and door
      open to the yard.

I looked in the still mirrors, breathed in
      long living room
no longer curtained but for sheers,
      cane furniture unfixed.

I put down my purse on her upstairs bed
      in case an embryonic
thought still rested there
      on white hobnail spread.

In this house she'd hosted, teetotaled, raised,
      letter-wrote, and scrubbed,
got trapped under the porch, mourned
      in the back lot dead-end road,

stood up to fry the chicken, make the coffee,
        salad, shrimp, and on more than
one occasion, ironed out the linen
        of what is true.

I had a chance, but my pride
        had such velocity I lied and said
I didn't lurk among her books, ashamed
        how little heaven I had made.

A new tinge is on her eye. Or call it a rind, like the covering of a washed cheese containing the reek of it. A hollow glare from stone-eyed gargoyles or dull glint of disused silverware. In the famine when God provided bread they called it *manna*, which means *What is it?* Each day arriving with the dew: gray light, gray air, gray everything. The orange cooler on her stoop (to receive the medicine or a daily meal) the only square of color.

BREAD OF HEAVEN

Given with this day also what is needed to get through it
If my friend would bring her little son to me

I'd give him lunch and a nap while she goes for help
Instead I'm driving by her house to spy the empty pool

Scorched grass my ruinous etiquette not wanting to intrude
I go on arranging the dianthus and looking under pews

One summer off the same vacant street
I was the only one who saw a man's anguished looks

Staining his bespoke shirt and hands held out terribly wrong
I always say *if there's anything I can do*

But today is not convenient
Having to meet her with groceries in the parking lot

Before I knew anyone who lived here the trees
Seemed lush and quieter and all the houses lamplit

With reading chairs fine thread sheets the closets
Ranged with goods as if on stockroom shelves

I had seen her shot of hope
Knuckling through the drunk day straight or lacquered

On the bench for afternoon either way the same
Wanting no part of brutal silence held by restaurant couples

She could've been steeped in sweet girls bringing
Casseroles and dresses but her proclivities always with the ballast

Of a darker severalty of coffee and exhaust
Choosing to be wholly improvised and at times exultant

Holding strong the sweet shambolic urges
That always need a staving off again until first light.

SHE VISITS ME

Reetika Vazirani (1962–2003)

Each day I flutter awake   in the tilled
world my friend   successfully imagined
leaving   while her little son

made   macaroni necklaces
at day camp   her mind slanted
away   the father had not

spoken   when she'd shown a copy
of the sonogram   seeded blackpearl
knew the depths   her list

of lilies   middle July   still wearing
the newsboy cap   carrying a patchwork
purse   the lab notebook

she always wrote in   meat   rice
melon   filling his sweet belly
cherries   salmon   broccoli

she had taken vitamins   averted
her eyes near knives   knocked
on doors   tried to borrow a Bible

she took him with her   cannot
let my own mind   rest
the small body she had   so lovingly

bathed and cared for   carried
I would see her   just once again
walking   through the palace

of an ordinary   grocery store
hurrying toward me   waving
bringing him   by the hand

PRESENT

Deborah Digges (1950–2009)

How could you refuse it
on the very verge of spring

when in another hour fury, grief
might ease off enough, allow

quick passage through, climbing down
in say, a cactus garden, angling into light

around adobes where you could
have rented rooms—but

the lost are like this: foster mothers, night
nurses for the lives of others, not their own—

you tore your page out, like the woman who
jumped from the *Mayflower* before her party

went ashore—the white oaks soaked and
fallen, failed in the same place I now look.

You gave your son a wonderful childhood,
as he wrote himself on the last page

of the sympathy book. How can we know
the number who have loved us, or how

few—*you shall not kill* applies
also to the self, though everywhere I meet

discouragements to an inquiring further,
drowsing deep in brief recursive red-flesh

woodlet days—*you shall not kill the apples*
up from the ground and tasting so good.

TAKING ORDERS

We left our husbands and baby sons and left our lives
crowded with objects and petty chores

and ran for the forest without catching sight
of any shepherds on the hill.

Particulars are constantly thrown into attention,
into opposition with the tidy nursery;

dust mites will always take the carpet
and lambs will have their lettuces.

Giving up requires commitment,
a complete ascetic focus. Both total

selflessness and selfishness take practice, practice
to act as the great men. And the women,

who kneel upon the cool tile floor, wedded not
to rite but to the untied feeling just before

and after it. I've been thinking maybe patience
is just laziness, in a different guise,

and remembrance is for piling in the cloud
in secure locations, never to see again.

I like going to the cafeteria
with my philosopher friend, choosing

some of this and some of that, renouncing
the world little by little, here and there.

FORGETFUL GREEN

There among heirloom tomatoes
    twigged on the short path I
disappeared from screened porch
    to divagate, to make it last,

the ox-eyed gloriosa, sweet alyssum,
    early dinner, black-eyed peas and
all that dusky sunset, incomparable heat,
    mare's nest of the indefinite.

I was diffident, dawdling on the path,
    betwixt—when every thread
in my dress, every cell of my skin
    became a sudden declaration

for the tending—this night the last
    supper, had to be, knowing here
was goodness, but (and) time to go:
    a charge so clear it blessed

the road's edge where I stood
    and the honeysuckle there
and all my subsequent, at times
    wretched, wanderings.

COME HERE WEATHER OF LOVE AND LET ME LOOK AT YOU

Frances Frost (1905–1959)

A mother left her toddler daughter
and her baby son, left her parents
to look after them when she went rolling

under the fence, wanting to belong
more deeply to her self, as a body
to a grave, or a rabbit springing

down the lane looking for lost fellows,
found frozen in a warren in the snow.
She called the fears, and then fears

came: bobcat, eagle, coyote, snake,
and the bare hearth when she washed up
home again, her boy now ten, no place

to get warm, nor outlive what's foolish
(though impossible not) to dwell on, finding
her threadbare cardigan in the windward shed.

Back to nights pouring milk, bringing
a serving dish again, getting them through
the drifts she knew about, knew too well,

returned from sunny ports brought low. She lost
the baby book, her daughter became a nun.
While she was gone her mother beat her son.

CREATE IN ME A CLEAN HEART, O GOD
—Psalm 51:10

The thing I did for sorrow was silence.
The thing I did for sorrow,
the thing I did,
the silence.

I thought when replacing the pillow
under the sleeping girl's head
it's been a while
since kindness.

When my mother was sick
I didn't go
I rolled over in my own bed
I thought she wanted

to be alone,
alone how I like to be
to keep my misery.
There's not much overlap

in what we understand,
no guard against unloving
sticks piled up, the thatched
huts, my ingratitude.

BLUEBIRD OF HAPPINESS®

The glass,
from pure white sand
of northeast Arkansas,
turned a lucent blue
by copper oxide added
in the molten stage, cooled
into this keepsake
figurine of friendly
message: contentment, good
health, spring—the perfect
inexpensive, inoffensive
gift, signed and dated
by a craftsman in 1989.
One small object traveled
well, almost never
noticed sitting high
up on a shelf, collecting
dust wherever it was
moved, benign but true
attendant at the passing
through the minutes, witness
to the rapids rushing
down from melting at great
altitudes and at times,
the going under. It shows
therefore a willingness: to feed
the ranges to a river, to start
again, become the glass with large
and noticeable grains in it.
To find a way out of the eddy
at the broad rebellious river's

mouth, and to make a ripple
in the highly straitened
rage (*Why can't you be satisfied!?*)
that washed me here.

.

LAND-AND-SEA

I like to swim out till I can't swim more
Until it's hard to get my breath and in gasping have work to do
Get back to shore
I don't want to tell you about the girl
Lying abed, my head beside hers
On the white pillow eyes white she said I have not prayed
I have barely ever done that I said don't worry I have done that for you
I have included you in all the days of my life
All days have been good for praying though it's hard to believe
That's all God wants
Shouldn't He want more in return for all this swanning around in the breeze
Feeling easy in the body
So animal, so wry
I love the purple inside oyster shells but haven't done a thing to help them
Nothing we can do to earn the mainsail beauty, given every day
And the lifting sea.

Call it *May of Spectacular Breezes,* best month of the atmosphere, loved excessively and afresh when walking out from the garage, a perfection such that everyone throws windows open, even my neighbors, where screams shriek out today through the upstairs screen, not only pain but *No more! No more.* All the other girls in school when the home health nurse brings packages of silver foil. One drug kills her appetite, another makes her eat. The mother has learned to administer anything, to bring in whatever appears at the door: small bottles of holy water and healing oil, a sprig of lily of the valley on Mother's Day. When the girl turned eleven, I slipped a Bible into the box of birthday gifts. I had hesitated, not wanting to offend the girl and her father, who do not believe. And the priest said *you don't ever have to apologize for Jesus* is what the priest said.

I HAVE LET THINGS SLIP

I could be wrong about the incarnadine
      jewelry of these tulips—deep-streaked
as if risen from a flood—as salve for a mind blowing off

in slight wind (tickseed, cotton boll, so much fluff).
      From childhood's porous province comes a hot
and stealthy flowering—broken by, yet seeking such.

I should have asked for an indifference, as tree or cloud.
      Or to have sooner been the woman almost ready
in the girl. Everyone seemed to know but me, that the passion

means a suffering, that words we use are seeded
      with an earlier sense, that all the eggs a girl
will have are present in her infant ovaries.

And that outcomes are often manifest long before
      the setting out: along with gold
and frankincense was myrrh for preparing a shroud.

CORTÈGE

Damned elegant graybrick house
thought about so much it owns me
—potent, plenary—

(waiting on prom night for a corsage)
(song in the body cannot get out)

I loved for no good reason
a flag ripping across stone steps,
spark and schooner; loved its mastery

of wind; loved the tennis-watching
uncles under blanket covers, gone. Gone
my August my fairway my good skin.

(girl is to house as song is to body)

Yelling at the internist:
what's an idiot *student* doing here
when my friend is *dying*?

And love, those white and purple flags
flapping on the hearse,
the absolute zero of graveside.

BROUGHT IN SAFETY TO THIS NEW DAY

Quietly the eggs
waited in the fridge

while we were half a world
away, waited in our house
under all this snow—

I did not inhabit our vacation
the way I had intended

so when I got home the snowfall
took on a wishful
tinge of tropical, adding

brilliance to the drift softening
the stone wall—then someone

came on business from the town
and when I returned to the window
that hint was gone—

I worry time may come to end
this way, blown.

LAST NIGHT'S AIR KISSES

At the party, our crash of facial bones
(zygomatic, mine around the eye,

maxilla, his, beneath the upper lip)
set off a *zzzt* of unhappy shock—

I should have left then,
covered too thinly by living skin,

overtaken by the rude extravagance
of food, the powder room too fine to use,

a guest's perfume (the one who whispered
she was glad for bruises because they proved

she lived with passion and was still worth
fighting for). For a while I feigned an interest

in the friendly, not needing more from them,
standing on the rug noticing a small blue truck

some toddler must have left, the only amulet
I'd keep—from childhood's hour I have known

I am best alone, last in the pool for the lifesavers'
test, or at the picnic, passing an egg from spoon to

spoon down a line of kids in bathing suits, loath
to trust myself (in brittle vial) to a bunglesome crowd.

APOSTASY, FAILED

Dry air and the dry edge of body meet,
the dying edge, in the din and slide
of my voluble tongue, spilling past thirsts.

It is right at last to admit
those wishes I was vigilant with, guarded
against, beat back like crows from the field.

But when I wave my arms to beckon them
home, they're too far gone to come in, flown
to flecks in unleavened sky. In vain I try

to taste the wine, pressed
with a crush of cloth to my lips—no, I can't
remember why I loved them so

(the wine and those exquisite, banished birds)
so much that I denied (denied, denied)
loving them, all my life.

MAGPIES IN ASPENS

In vicinity of treeline
I am inert and raging as family silver

tarnished in stuck drawers.
Late summer hikers find back bowls.

Magpies' ascending cry: *unhappy.*

All would be better with some hot
strong coffee, which could be had

by walking easily through
the swinging doors of the saloon

if I had still a filament of strength,
if half the maidens had not already

filled their lamps with oil, if sunflower heads
did not tip so rudely out of pitchers

where the lovely sip their wine—
if there weren't so many possible ways

to go astray, none settled on so far—
for who has not required some small sight

more than circumstance
could give? Should she not be praised?

IN THE SECOND HALF OF LIFE

You could make the necessary arrangements to be
walking there again, drinking from the old well
under dogwoods breaking open strong as parachutes,
to savor blossoms without fruit; you could find a small
house with a few big rooms, make a friend or two
who'd swing on the porch then fade into a comfortable
distance. You could live within an ocean view, put limpets
in a jar. You could, with no remorse, read quietly
in your room. Refuse to worry about hurting anyone.
Throw something on the fire besides yourself to cause
a merry blaze; work so everything's heightened, raised
to best translation, brightest hue; you could sleep more,
stay in touch, become a vegetarian. You could pine
for solitude and then complain of loneliness.

EVEN THE GLADIOLI

January first, home in the dark
like a coin caught in coat hem—

it must've slipped through the hole
in my pocket down into the lining

where a hand can't reach, like a jewel
sewn into garments by war-torn refugees—

oh I'm rattling about, in the old mental act
of crossing Main and Pine in a fine

light rain, past versions of my self to step
across—penniless in the gallery

with grand views of the bay, lifting
a wineglass floating gold, devouring

plates of beef—house sitting when the king's
away, last light listening in the breach,

holding the gaudy vase of glads
a man spent his last dollars on, my birthday—

I trap the minutes far from there, pretend
to be no longer subject to such wild

irregularity, but fired and glazed, a finished
self, chosen and held, like a prize at the fair.

FURLOUGH

On the nightstand the corpse of a pear,
a whole immobile March,

shuddered awake each four A.M. black
as a whistle—the cold-sweat instant

no hint of who she is—to go out
to the dovecote, throw birds to air, gone

with luff and lift. The blue ache
a sky all for itself, as joy is.

Feel how thin the lattice is
that holds us, fretwork of rotting calm.

WHEN I WAS ALONE

When I was alone
I ate only popcorn, stayed unwashed,
roamed my house as a cave
and I the lone greedy inhabitant—
left to my own twists became
part animal, all narcissist—I
replayed the same movie, sharpened
each pencil, ransacked the attic,
drank scotch from a thimble, kept
indulging dizzy whims until keeping
at it led to some further liberation—derived
from a solitary listening—one
full long day of following myself
wherever I might lead, the paths of excess
commanding every cell of my attention,
and when it was over I went out on the patio
and that's when I thought about my babies
growing up, and the brigade of trees standing watch.

In sweeter soil or milder rain, trellised along another road
I'd be—but here am I, staked up alone beside your fence.
As you come and go along the path, lady with a worried
look, I wish you'd sit by me a fraction to forget the rose is
sick. When you return with pizza box, pink lemonade,
dreaming again her appetite, the crumpled packed-down
hope of petals is opening inside. *The sick rose*, I reply.

DOG DAYS

Scrambling eggs
this clammy Sunday morning
no one knows I'm still here.
Even ghosts leave me alone.

As I stand in my slip
at the ironing board, an odd
grief comes steaming:
brief seizure, storm
on the moon. A belligerent little disbelief.

I try to catch it on my tongue.

Steam rises and follows
to the backyard, anonymous,

while inside the cooling blouse and skirt
cotton together on the dumb valet,
the soft cloth blue like sails

from a distant summer's taut and shimmer,
somewhere beyond the battery.

In the fish pond
orange goldfish float up, meaty as fists.

Standing in the sweaty grass
I weigh a bloated tomato in each hand,

buoy them up
without breaking their stems.

PRAYER THAT STARTS IN THE EYE OF A BIRD

It sees magnetic fields and ultraviolet light. As it flies, horizons stay precise. It picks up small sticks and thatches them, makes a lining of grass. It pursues the loosely strung, as if hunting for lacewings. Each night the prayer takes up a constant thread, aloft above the neighborhood in sight of other guides, in love with the vista of everyone, put to bed in perfect wool.

SELF-PORTRAIT WITH AMERICAN CROWS

Telling lies, wasting time, thinking
no one else keeps promises
as close as I—crows fly in

and convene on the elm, an insistence
of wingspan, black-black-green.
The effort of cawing racks

their whole bodies, swaying
the top of the tree. I know crows
keep the law. I know fate will be

my friend, bear out
my diffidence, live in the void
with my deluded attitude

of permanence, and everyday
bliss: sitting on the stoop
with my little boys

in the shadow of the elm,
stuffing ourselves with potato chips
as everything turns to glory.

NOTES

In "Fox in the Yard," *if Thou art so lovely in thy creatures, how exceeding ravishing Thou must be* is from the writings of Henry Suso (1295–1366).

"Don't Worry" has St. Julian of Norwich in mind.

In "The Forest," *as often a life does not begin at its beginning* is from Françoise Gilot's book *Life with Picasso*.

In "Present," *you tore your page out* is paraphrased from John Berryman.

"I Have Let Things Slip" is part of a line from Sylvia Plath's "Tulips."

The title "Brought in Safety to This New Day" is paraphrased from *The Book of Common Prayer*.

ACKNOWLEDGMENTS

The Christian Century: "Land-and-Sea"

Colorado Review and *Verse Daily*: "Furlough"

The Cresset: "I Have Let Things Slip," "Present," and "She Visits Me"

Dogwood: A Journal of Poetry and Prose: "When I Was Alone"

Fusion: "The Girl in Us" (as "Avenue of the Stars") and "Self-Portrait with American Crows" (also featured on the Mass Poetry website as a Poem of the Moment, 2015)

Image: "Create in Me a Clean Heart, O God" and "Crewelwork"

Letters: "Exile from the Kingdom of Ordinary Sight"

Massachusetts Cultural Council Website: "The Great Mirror" (as "Ecstatic Neighborhood")

Mid-American Review: "In the Second Half of Life"

Poetry Society of America, Robert H. Winner Award: "Present" and "Taking Orders" (as "Practice)," were part of a group of poems that won the 2010 award.

Salamander: "Brought in Safety to This New Day," "Dog Days," and "Taking Orders" (as "Practice")

Smartish Pace: "Bread of Heaven," "Elm" (as "Columbia Gorge"), and "Forgetful Green"

Southern Poetry Review: "Bluebird of Happiness®"

The Southern Review: "Apostasy, Failed" and "Cortège"

Spoon River Poetry Review: "In Which the Bread Crumbs Were Eaten by Birds"

Tusculum Review: "Safe in the Ground" and "The Youngest Ocean"

Heartfelt thanks to Allison Joseph, Jon Tribble, the Crab Orchard Series in Poetry, and everyone at Southern Illinois University Press. And thank you to those who gave essential comments or otherwise tended these poems: Sandra Beasley, Lucie Brock-Broido and all her summer poets, Brian Burt, Amy M. Clark, the Colrain Manuscript Conference, Jennifer S. Flescher, the Reverend Cathy George, Kirun Kapur, the Reverend Margery Kennelly, Cecily Parks, Mike Perrow, Beth Woodcome Platow, Lynne Potts, Jessica Stern, Erin Trahan, Jonathan Weinert, and Kate Westhaver. To my dear family and my amazing boys. And as ever, to Jack Goldsmith.